WEALTH

Accumulating Money, Building Wealth and Staying Rich Through Sound Financial Management and Time-Tested Strategies.

ZACHARY D. WEST

Introduction

I want to thank you and congratulate you for buying the book, *"WEALTH: Accumulating Money, Building Wealth and Staying Rich through Sound Financial Management and Time-Tested Strategies"*.

This book contains proven steps and strategies on how to acquire wealth through sound financial management, establishing stable cash flow systems and preparing yourself for the riches and issues that will come ahead.

This book is a comprehensive guide to help you achieve a state of wealth. You will first learn why it is best to go for wealth as early as now. Next, you will learn how you can increase the amount of cash that flows into your coffers. You will then learn how you can properly manage your money so you won't make any unnecessary expenses. The next part will talk about how investments can change the game for you.

Last but not least, this book will talk about the common mistakes people commit when trying to get rich and how you can improve yourself to become more ready for wealth.

Thanks again for buying this book, I hope you enjoy it!

Chapter 1 - Why the Best Time to Build Wealth Is Now

"My favorite time frame is forever"
- Warren Buffett

"Get rich or die trying" - a popular quote by Curtis "50 Cent" Jackson, one of the music industry's most successful hip-hop artists. More than just being a mantra to live by, a lot of people actually live in this state. People are willing to do whatever it takes to secure their finances now and in the future. Of course, doing this is easier said than done. In fact, a lot of people live their lifetimes without reaching the state of permanent financial stability, hence, they "die trying".

There are many ways to ensure that you will have more than enough money for yourself, your family, and possibly your kin in the future. One way to swing the odds to your favor is to build your fortune right now.

Many people put off doing the steps to getting rich because they have this mentality that they have all the time in the world to make enough money to live comfortably in the future. While success stories where people attain financial stability late in their lives exist, the odds of getting this done are considerably smaller compared to starting at a younger age.

Aside from this, there is no way to tell what's going to happen in the future. In the future, it is possible that you will lose your job, your business opportunities may dry up, or the local stock market may crash, just to name some possible scenarios. If the breaks don't go your way, you can find yourself in financial ruin at any moment.

Considering this, the best time to build wealth is right now. Regardless of your age, your source of income, or your family standing, it helps to make the necessary efforts to acquire wealth now and not next time. Here are some of the reasons why starting now will help you increase your odds of building enough wealth to sustain you and your family for the rest of your life.

1. It gives you more time to do the necessary steps.

As you will find out on the following chapters, you have to take multiple steps to ensure you'll have enough wealth. Given the number of steps you need to take, the sooner you do them, the better your chances of actually getting it done. You have to remember that getting rich is a process, and you can't just expect results to come out in an instant. Because of this, you need to give yourself enough time to perform all the steps necessary to build a strong financial foundation. Give yourself enough time to get rich and you're more likely than not to be rewarded for your efforts.

2. It helps you build the right habits

You need to have the right habits if you want to build a fortune. Just about every financial expert out there will tell you this. In fact, several topics in this book will actually focus on working on your financial habits. It also takes time to master something for it to become a habit. As such, your chances of building the right habits also increase significantly. Starting right now will improve your chances in mastering the right habits for achieving and maintaining wealth.

3. You can never tell what can happen in the future

This is one reality everyone has to face. One can never be too sure about what will happen in the future. One moment you can have about everything you wish for. The next moment, all that you have can be gone. The point is that in this world, there are simply no guarantees. If you defer the opportunity to make your finances grow, you may miss the chance to do it altogether. The best time to do something is now because you'll never know what the future holds.

4. You get more opportunities to accumulate riches

As mentioned in the previous point, you'll never know how many opportunities you get to accomplish the things you want to do. Because of this, it is simply a *must* to make the most out of the chances you get. Aside from taking every possible advantage and opportunity given to you, it's also vital to put yourself into positions in which you get access to these opportunities. The best way to do it is to start building your riches today. That way, you are putting the odds on your side for getting multiple chances to maximize your net worth.

If you want to create a fortune, the best time to start is right now. At this moment, the clock is ticking. The time you delay ends up as wasted time, giving you fewer opportunities to accomplish the things you need to do. The next thing you know, your window closed already. I recommend that if you want to build your wealth, you have to start now. In the next chapters of this book, you'll learn about the various techniques and strategies you can use to earn money, create sustainable cash flows, and manage expenses properly.

Chapter 2 - Earn Money, Build Wealth

"If you want to be successful, there is absolutely no way around hard, hard work."

- Arnold Schwarzenegger

While only a few people will admit this, earning enough money is crucial in this time and age. While money does not guarantee happiness or even a good life, it does help to make life better. It helps you (and your loved ones) get your needs adequately and get more and better life opportunities. The problem is that a lot of people don't know how to earn money the right way. You have to earn money the right way to ensure that you'll have more than enough in the bank as you ride into the sunset. Here are some tips to live by to earn money and build wealth.

1. Find a niche

Regardless of what money-making methods you use, it is important to find your niche. After all, if you don't fit in, there's no way you can prosper there (and in effect rack up the cash at a high rate). There are multiple considerations to take into account when you're finding a niche. First, it has to fit in your interests. If you like what you're doing, learning and taking action becomes much easier.

Second, you've got to have the skills for it. If you have the knack for a particular field, you're more likely than not to achieve success. Third, it has to be rewarding. If it does not provide you either progress or satisfaction, it's probably not the right field for you. Not all people find their niche, but those who do will, more likely than not, end up successful. Warren Buffett famously stays within his 'circle of competence' when making investments. Find your own.

2. Work hard

It's been said time and again that success almost always end up being a question of effort. If you want to build your riches, it is almost imperative to work hard for it. This is especially so when you are just getting started. In your chosen career, you have to always give your best shot to ensure that you are always in the best position to succeed. Give both your time and effort to create earning opportunities. Take time to learn the nuances of your chosen profession, as well as to explore potential options to rack up more cash, assets and opportunities.

3. Work smart

Some say that these days, working hard is not enough. You also have to work smart. Working smart puts emphasis on both precision and efficiency. Such an approach allows you to maximize your earnings and accomplishments while using minimal resources like time, effort and money. This is the route taken by all great organizations and individuals, and you need to take the same approach as well. To do this, take time to learn the best and most effective approaches. Also, make an effort to maximize all of your resources. That way, you increase your chances of acquiring wealth while still having the freedom to do the things you want.

4. Always seek out opportunities

One of the keys to achieving success in virtually everything you do, is to *actively* seek for opportunities to succeed. While some are lucky enough to stumble on something and achieve success beyond their wildest imagination, the odds of doing that are low. In other words, it is still better to place your fate in your own hands. Actively seek for chances to make money, investments and make personal improvements. This is your best bet to having a better chance to achieve all your goals. Of course, not all opportunities that you see are right for you (more on this later), but you can't usually find what you don't even try to seek.

5. Always consider entrepreneurship

While having any kind of job and actively earning money is always good, this is almost always not enough to ensure that you have sufficient cash flow for the rest of your life. Keep in mind that you physically cannot work forever. Consider earning opportunities wherein you produce money even when you don't do anything. This is what financial advisers call "passive income". Build your passive income sources, and the best way to do this is by being a successful entrepreneur.

6. Invest

Investing is one of the best ways to earn money both immediately and in the long run. An entire chapter is dedicated to making investments so I won't spill the beans too much just yet. Of course, it's not enough to just make investments. You have to make the right investments, because any form of investment can be disastrous for your finances when done the wrong way. This aspect of earning money will be saved for later, but hold this thought as early as now: you'll need to make the right investments to build and maintain your wealth.

The first step in amassing wealth is, of course, to earn money. However, just because you are earning money, even large amounts, that doesn't mean that you are on your way towards getting rich. The key to getting rich is to find the best ways to gain income both actively and passively, and invest the difference. Follow the tips here and you will be on your way to making more money and becoming closer to accomplishing your desired state of wealth.

Chapter 3 - Learn How to Properly Manage your Budget and Expenses

"Don't save what is left after spending. Spend what is left after saving"

- Warren Buffett

There are 2 sides of the coin when it comes to increasing your net worth. The part that's always talked about in this equation is increasing the amount of money you earn. After all, who doesn't want to earn lots of cash? Having a ton of money not only makes you technically rich; it is also a great way to somewhat improve your personal worth. However, the not-so-glamorous side of increasing your net worth is keeping your expenses to a minimum.

The sad thing is that not many people know how to manage their budget and expenses. In fact, some don't even care about this aspect until it's too late. This chapter will tell you how you can do it and avoid the pitfalls of financial mismanagement.

1. Learn to respect your money

Remember that you need to take control of money, not the other way around. Of course, that is much easier said than done. The first step to managing your expenses properly is to have respect for your money. Understand that your money is powerful, so powerful that it can control a lot of your daily activities. When you realize that taking control of your finances will help you achieve financial freedom sooner than later, you open yourself up to amassing wealth.

2. Never underestimate small amounts

Value your money, no matter how small it is. This applies to both your savings and your profits. When you are building up your fortune, every penny counts, so never underestimate small amounts. Saving up even just a minimal amount of your daily income can translate to major savings in the long run. Also, making investments that yield passive income, even if this yield is seemingly miniscule, will translate to potentially big savings in time. When you are budgeting, even the small amounts matter - always keep that in mind.

3. Learn to save money

Your parents and other old folks have probably told you that you should start saving money. I recommend that you heed their advice, regardless of what your standing in life is. Think long-term when managing your finances. The money you save will allow you to achieve financial freedom sooner. You can use the money you save on future expenses, making investments, and establishing extra financial streams. What's more, if you save enough money earlier, you'll have more time to do the things you want and spend your time with the people who matter to you.

4. Avoid making debts you cannot commit to

If you are trying to achieve financial freedom, debts can turn out to be among your biggest obstacles. For sure, you have heard how debts have sent countless people into bankruptcy. Having debts can put a dent on your savings, earnings, or both. The same is true for other financing options such as loans, mortgages and installments. There are some situations wherein availing of these financing options is a must, but you have to do it in a sustainable manner. It is best to avoid making debts, especially if you cannot commit to paying them.

5. Differentiate between needs and wants

This is another fundamental aspect of financial management that's often overlooked by both the rich and the poor. Know how to differentiate between your needs and wants. Prioritizing your wants and desires, often as a means of providing personal gratification, can turn out as a potentially disastrous habit. Some people will even go as far as justifying their desire as a need, or at least as a means to reward their efforts. While it's perfectly okay to fulfill your indulgences every now and then, it's never a good thing if it's starting to eat into your savings and/or your funds for daily necessities and expenses. In the words of investment titan Warren Buffett – "if you buy things you do not need, soon you will have to sell things you need".

6. Make proper money decisions

Making the right decisions with your money can go a long way in improving your bottom line. This applies to both budgeting and spending. When you make a conscious effort to make better decisions with your money, you put yourself in a better position to become wealthier. Living within your means allows you to manage your expenses better. Prioritizing your long-term financial stability over your short-term wants will help you build rather than break your finances. When you make a conscious effort to formulate the right financial decisions, almost everything else will fall into place.

Once you know how to spend and manage your money the right way, you don't need to have a stratospheric amount of money to accomplish your mission. When you change the way you use your finances, you put yourself in the position to get wealthy sooner rather than later. Furthermore, it helps you keep your money, even as you advance in age and stop working.

Chapter 4 - Make Smart Investments

"Someone is sitting in the shade today because someone planted a tree a
long time ago."

- Warren Buffett

It is mentioned earlier that while working for your money (as an employee,
a self-employed person, or as a businessman) is great, this is a very limited
means of earning your keep. This is because you can only work for so long
before you start getting old, less energetic or less mentally capable. At some
point, you have to consider making your money work for you. This is what
you call earning passive income. The best way to get this vital source of
extra money is to make investments. It is not enough to invest; you also
have to invest intelligently. This chapter will focus on the things you must
do to ensure that you make smart investments.

1. Make investing a habit

The world's richest people and the best financial advisers will tell you that
turning investing into a habit is always a good idea. You need to learn how
to set aside at least a portion of your income as reserve funds for future
investments. Turning investment into a personal habit will not just provide
you with enough funds to complete the right deals as soon as they emerge,
but it will eventually help you create enough financial streams so you'll have
enough financial breathing room in the future. As a rule of thumb, it is
recommended to save at least 10-25% of your income.

2. Actively look for investment opportunities

There are all kinds of investment opportunities out there that will help you create substantial savings and help you earn piles of cash in a passive manner. You can invest in the stock market, establish or buy into a private business, deposit money in a high interest bank account with (rare these days however!), or invest in real estate. There are different pros and cons in making specific investments, so make sure to check them out before throwing in your hard-earned money. Learn the nuances of your chosen investment avenue and be skeptical of all people selling you a dream; all investments should start with you looking for these opportunities yourself.

3. Take a long-term perspective

The conflicting nature of most types of investing can be counter-intuitive to people looking for quick cash – most of the time, this approach is not for those who are looking for instant gratification. While some investments bear fruit almost overnight, the reality is that most investments don't dramatically explode in value right away. Most accumulate value over a long period of time, while others provide small yet substantial profit. Making investments sometimes means making short-term sacrifices. However, should things go your way, it will pay off handsomely.

4. Take time to learn investing techniques

There are different ways to invest, with each method having its own distinct pros and cons. Regardless of what approach you take, it is important to note that you should consider investing as a skill. It is something that you can work on and something you can definitely excel at. There are specific approaches that work, and mastering these approaches will prove critical in achieving success. Take time to learn about the rules, strategies, trends, and all those other factors. These will help you get into the best position to make the most out of your investments.

5.   Learn when to let go of specific investments

As important as it is to acquire investments, you also need to learn when to let go of these same investments. There are different reasons why you should let go of particular investments. It could be that their value has significantly declined and will decline even further with time. It can also be that times have changed so much that it's simply isn't smart any longer to hold on to it. It is important to stay objective and know when to let go of investments that are simply doing badly. A lot of people get emotionally attached to investments – and the decision that went along with investing in the first place. They get blinded from reality, and cannot let go. It may be somewhat hard to accept that you made a mistake, but it happens to everyone. Learn from it and move on.

6.   Be open to changes

To invest, you need to be open to change. It is a fact that trends in various investments are constantly changing. That said, you need to make the necessary efforts to keep up with the times. For example, while investing on trusted platforms is always a good idea, some new platforms actually offer great returns. Also, depending on the economic climate, some assets will increase in value while others decline. Lastly, some strategies that used to be effective in the past become obsolete later on, and vice versa. You have to be open to changes when you are in the field of investment.

Learning how to invest is one of the fundamental ways to ensure that you'll have more than enough wealth when all is said and done. Follow the tips in this book to ensure that you'll invest the right way. Becoming an investor often involves a trial-and-error process. It is best to learn from trying and from the mistakes you have committed. The best way to escape potential failure is to learn as much as you can. This is where your knowledge of proper investing technique will come into the picture.

Chapter 5 – Money Mistakes to Avoid

"Learn from the mistakes of others. You can't live long enough to make
them all yourself."

- Eleanor Roosevelt

So far, this book has focused on the things that you should do to acquire
wealth. However, there are times when predicting success or failure is not
just about what you should do; it is also about what you shouldn't do.
There are some mistakes done by people from different walks of life that
put them in a situation wherein they can't build their wealth. In fact, some
make mistakes that take them only closer to bankruptcy. This chapter will
focus on some of the most common mistakes people commit when it
comes to managing their finances. Take note of each of these. Should you
be making any of these, make the necessary efforts to fix them.

1. Don't become stagnant

Stagnancy is the enemy of anyone who wants to achieve sustained and long-
term success. This is especially applicable for those who already had the
taste of success and accomplishment. The problem with human nature is
that once we achieve a goal, we start resting on our laurels and stop doing
what took us to success in the first place. Eventually, this will either cause
you to stop gaining more wealth or even take away all that you have worked
for. As such, it is important that you don't become stagnant. Keep
improving your financial streams, continue looking for investments, and
maintain good spending habits.

2. Don't ignore discretionary income

Discretionary income is defined as the portion of your cash flow apart from what you use for your daily necessities. While having discretionary income is always great, it is how you use it that determines its overall usefulness. Most people make the mistake of spending this portion of their funds for luxuries, vices and other things that don't really add up to your net worth. While spending on these things is not necessarily bad, it's not a good idea to spend all your discretionary income on these things. It would be wiser to use a higher percentage of this income for savings, investments and acquisition of actual assets.

3. Don't make unnecessary risks and investments

One misconception of some moneyed individuals is that making any investment is better than making none at all. A lot of people lose great amounts of money by taking too many risks and making bad investments. If you are going to make an investment, it is important to be sure about it. Evaluate first if this is something that you can succeed on. Study the nuances of your investment and how you can make that investment work. Check if it's the type of investment that will make your bottom-line better, not worse, in the long run. Investing is a risk in itself and there are no guarantees for success, but that risk has to be a calculated one.

4. Be selective in the people you work with

Establishing a good network is essential to succeed in just about anything. However, there are some people that you simply have to avoid. There are certain people you shouldn't work or make transactions with. You need to have the wisdom to discern which types of people you should not trust, especially when handling something as sensitive as your finances. When working with other people, prioritize working with those who are qualified for the task at hand and share the same vision as yours.

5. Don't let success get to your head

For most people, financial problems start not when they run out of savings or lose their sources of income; problems start because they get too comfortable with their savings or income. When their own success gets to their head, some people tend to have extravagant lifestyles, make financially unsound investments, and basically forget how to manage their money. This is where most financial problems start to emerge. As such, one good way to secure your finances is to not let your success get into your head.

6. Don't panic

Unless you win the lottery, you most likely won't get rich overnight. There will be some anxious moments from time to time. You may not be saving the amount of money that you expected, and the movement in the value of your assets is lower and slower than what you hoped for. When this happens, the last thing you want is to panic. Remember that earning wealth takes a long period of time. In such situations, what you need the most is patience and an open mind. Keep in mind that results don't always come instantly. You need to be objective enough to see if you'll need to adjust both your habits and approach. Still, don't panic.

Anyone can be prone to committing mistakes. One of the best ways to avoid (or at least lessen) them is to make a constant effort to avoid them.

The items mentioned in this chapter are just some of the most common mistakes people make while trying to become wealthy. Aside from following the tips mentioned here, take time to learn about other things that can go wrong so you will know how to avoid or at least make up for them.

Chapter 6 - Continuously Work on Yourself

"All of us have the power of choice. I choose to be rich, and I make that choice every day."

- *Robert Kiyosaki*

Earning a fortune goes beyond getting a high-paying job, making multiple investments, and becoming an expert in financial management. As experts would say, some people are built to handle the perks and pressures of wealth. Other people succumb to it and end up squandering their resources or worse. As such, to gain wealth and make it stick, you must become the person who can handle the demands of being wealthy.

To stay on top and continue building your wealth, you need to continuously work on yourself. This chapter will talk about the kind of approach you need to become the kind of person tailor-made to be wealthy for life.

1. Turn successful people into your inspiration

People who achieved success before us serve as a blueprint on how we can achieve success ourselves. Their accomplishments should serve as your benchmark on how you should handle things in your life. Following this logic, it would be wise to learn about the lives of people who have successfully created their own wealth. See how they were able to achieve success, overcome the struggles they faced along the way, and the winning approaches they used to get to where they are now. Learn from the lives of the best and use these as your inspiration to achieve the same in yours. Tony Robbins, the world-famous motivational speaker puts it like this: "If you want to be successful, find someone who has achieved the results you want and copy what they do – you'll achieve the same results".

2. Learn from the mistakes of others

The stories of others go beyond just looking at the positives. As humans, of course, people make mistakes. Some make mistakes that can be impossible to reverse, but often than not, there is a way out of it. It is important to learn from the mistakes others have made. When you do so, it will only help you to get better. Not only will it help you avoid making the same mistakes in the future, but it will also give you an idea on how to deal with potential issues that may come your way. Ray Dalio, manager of the largest hedge fund in the world argues that "There's an incredible beauty to mistakes, because embedded in each is a puzzle, and a gem that could be obtained if solved i.e. a principle that could be used to reduce mistakes in the future". Now ponder that.

3. Always take time to evaluate yourself

Self-improvement can be quite a complex task. Of course, you'll have a hard time improving if you don't know about the things you still have to improve on. This is where the power of self-evaluation comes into the picture. Evaluate yourself from time to time to see how you are actually doing. It will help you recognize the things you are doing right while helping you identify things you can still improve on. The first step to self-development is self-evaluation. Do it whenever you can.

4. Work with others

Some people say that acquiring a fortune is a personal journey. To some degree, this is correct, because ultimately, you are the one responsible for your own fate. However, it will help your bottom line if you work with others. Having people skills and the ability to work with others is crucial for you to achieve not just wealth, but virtually anything in this world. Knowing how to work with others can make your life much easier, allowing you to earn wealth faster and make your operations more efficient. Also, working with others can help you expand your network, which can give you more potential opportunities down the road. Needless to say, working with others is crucial to achieving wealth. If you are interested in learning more about training your skills in leadership and self-confidence to help you succeed with people, check out my other works at the end of this book on the topic.

5. Realize that money should not define you

Some people are so obsessed with amassing wealth that it consumes just about every part of their being. At any point, this should never be the case. No matter how rich you may become, you should realize that money should not define you. A lot of people lose themselves (and the things that matter to them) because they are so absorbed with earning money. Others let money and the process of earning it dominates their lives. Money should never define who you are, no matter how much cash you have in your wallet or bank account.

6. Just keep going

Earning and maintaining wealth is a lifelong process. There are so many things to learn and experience out there. It is important to keep going. Having this mentality will help you achieve everything you want in life and more. Were you able to accomplish all your life goals? Keep moving forward. Do you feel like you can still accomplish more? Keep moving forward. Are you currently experiencing difficulties? Keep moving forward. It is important that regardless of where you stand at the moment, you just got to keep going.

Earning a fortune is certainly not going to be easy. You really have to be up to the challenge of getting wealthy and being wealthy. Fortunately, you can definitely be up to it and achieve the wealth you desire, no matter who you are, where you are from, and what you are doing. You just need to continually work on yourself, get better in different aspects of life, and become better in handling the day-to-day rigors associated with building and maintaining wealth.

Conclusion

Thank you again for buying this book!

I hope this book was able to help you learn everything you need to know about the process of building wealth! Use the tips and techniques mentioned here to earn more money, stick to your budget better, and learn the importance of investing.

Finally, if you enjoyed this book, then I'd like to ask you for a favor - would you be kind enough to leave a review for this book on Amazon? It'd be greatly appreciated!

Thank you and good luck!

Zachary D. West

Preview Of "Leadership: How to Be a Leader, Boost Your Business Skills and Influence People"

2. Communicating like a leader

Great leaders are excellent communicators. All your ideas will not matter if you do not know how to communicate them effectively to your followers. There are many types of communication that a leader needs to master.

First, you need to develop the ability to talk to a huge crowd. Most people are afraid of talking to large groups of people. If you develop this skill, you will have an advantage over your competition in leadership positions. Here is a process that you can follow on how to talk to big groups:

a.   Identify your objective for talking to the group

Always have an objective when you talk to a group. When you gather people to listen to you, you are using up their valuable time. Without a clearly stated objective, the meeting will have no direction. People may waste time talking about irrelevant topics.

b.   Create a message that accomplishes your objectives

If you are not used to communicating with groups of people, you need to prepare your message in advance so that you can practice it before delivering it to your target audience. This will increase your chances of delivering an authoritative message.

c.   …

Head to Amazon.com to find out more!!

Zachary D. West

Check Out My Other Books

Below you'll find some of my other books that are popular on Amazon and Kindle as well. Simply head to Amazon to check them out. Alternatively, you can visit my author page on Amazon to see other work done by me.

Confidence: How To Boost Your Self Confidence And Self Esteem, Turn Your Life Around And Be Confident In Any Situation.

Leadership: How To Be a Leader, Boost Your Business Skills and Influence People.

Positive Thinking: How to Change Your Negative Mindset on Life, Build the Habit of Positive Thoughts and Live a Happy and Successful .

Thank you!

www.ingramcontent.com/pod-product-compliance
Lightning Source LLC
Chambersburg PA
CBHW070428190526
45169CB00003B/1467